Twirlin'

A brief history of Twirlin'

The When The How and The Who

Kwesi Daniels
w/
James Felton Keith

THINK ENXIT PRESS | ENXIT GROUP

New York

2011

THINK ENXIT PRESS
Published and Edited by the Enxit Group

Enxit Group (USA) Limited Liability Company, 150 West 47th Street Suite 9F, New York, NY 10036, USA | SEMTAN Media Limited Liability Company, 28675 Franklin Rd. Suite 631, Southfield, MI 48034, USA| Think Enxit Inc. 25031 Chambley Dr., Southfield, MI 48034, USA

First Published in 2011 by The Enxit Group (USA) LLC
a member of The Enxit Group

Kwesi Daniels & James Felton Keith, 2011
Open rights reserved

Library of Congress Cataloging-in-Publication Data

Daniels, Kwesi & Keith, James Felton
A brief history of Twirlin': The When The How and The Who
http://twirlin.info

ISBN: 061543908X | EAN-13: 978-0615439082
1. History 2. American History 3. African American History

Printed in the United States of America

DESIGNED BY James Felton Keith

Without limiting the rights of the original author above, all parts of this publication may be reproduced, stored in or introduced into a retrieval system, or transmitted, in any form or by any means (electronic, mechanical, photocopy, recording or otherwise), without the prior written permission of both the author and the above publisher of this book.

The scanning, uploading, and distribution of this book via the Internet or via any other means without the permission of the publisher is legal and by no means punishable by law. Please purchase all authorized electronic editions and do not participate in or encourage electronic piracy of this material without adding due value in the process. Your support for the author is appreciated.

This book is dedicated the hobbyists making Twirlin' a habit.

Special thanks to the Masters: Damien (D-Fin) Finley; Deltric (Paco) Latham; Rod (Zorro)Moody; David K Boyd; Drew Brown; Kenneth O'Rourke; and Johnny Edwards.

Contents

Forward	i
PART ONE: The When	1
| A Brief History	3
PART TWO: The How	9
| How to…	10
Twirlin' Dictionary	11
Mechanics of Twirlin	15
2nd Count Revolutions	15
1st Count Revolutions	16
Windmills	18
Body Wrapping	20
PART THREE: The Who	23
| Interviews	25
D-Fin	27
David K Boyd	33
Kenny O'Rourke	37
Drew Brown	41
Paco Veela	51
Zorro	59
Kwesi Daniels	63
Johnny Blaze	69
SNOTY The First	81
About the Author	97

Forward

I still remember the YouTube hype that Kwesi created in 2006 just after he sent me an email with David Boyd's video that sparked the first viral Twirlin' recording. It almost seemed wrong, when remembering how I was taught to critique and share how I worked with the cane while back in Alabama. Ten years just flies by. When Kwesi first told me that he wanted to compile as many interviews as possible for a publication on Twirlin', I immediately thought "that is going to be difficult". Being on the inside, I knew that the few of us who were called *kanemaster* by others were more secretive about how we did, what we did, than any fraternity. It's a group of elite elitists. Few get in, and everyone on the inside is critical about anyone claiming that they are worthy. I know plenty of brothers that can Twirl, but the most famous of us would take the opportunity to pick out every flaw in their delivery.

Because Twirlin' is such a new thing...martial art, sport, skill set...(I've heard it referred to as each of those), everyone who we know as *kanemaster* lays claim to a set of tricks and styles as their own. That may be impossible for every master to do in the future. I've always been of the group that thought Twirlin' should be shared and recorded more than less, to inspire the next generation to do something even more innovative. But when we started out to make a *how to* video in late 2006, some of the brothers said that it was impossible to teach and that we were likely wasting our time. Of course they made some sense; however, the objective was never to transfer identical skills, but it was to provoke something new. When I was 20, I got a VHS of arguably the first big name in Twirlin', Mike "Dirty Red" Slider and a new (at that time) master named Rod "Zorro" Moody going at it in Atlanta, 1999. I don't Twirl like either of them, but they inspired me. Having acknowledged that during talks with the other brothers who make the cane look like it obeys their every thought, many of them remarked "everyone will just start doing my moves". That of course being said just after they've said, "I don't Twirl anymore"...LOL.

When I saw the roster of interviews that Kwesi had for this book project I immediately thought to myself that it wasn't everyone who should be represented. Then testimonies started to come in, and I thought he had something special that needed to be shown to everyone who cares about Twirlin'. What the responses to the interview questions won't tell anyone is that, we all talk...a lot...and that, there is some controversy over who is a master and who is not. Even some of the most well know names are being critiqued for their unique *sweetness*....that's my old slang...LOL. A few weeks before this publication there was a public rant on Facebook (of all places) between Paco and Drew Brown about who was great and who wasn't. I can't quote any of it because I missed it being taken down by a few minutes, after receiving an email and call.

Drew, for those of you who don't know, is a technician, a real student of the cane. He is also an acclaimed juggler. His style of Twirlin' is different, not any more superior or less, but different. There are some brothers older and younger than him that think his style is other-than, Twirlin'. Paco, in the same regard, is probably the most well-known down south for his unrivaled fluency with the cane. At Atlanta Greek picnic, it's almost a guarantee that he'll intimidate 99% of the younger brothers from even stepping on the stage. So, both of these guys skills and styles are formidable to state the very least.

It's necessary for all of the readers to understand that there is a culture within the group of Twirlers deemed, master. While we all acknowledge the others as being great, we'd rarely (I've never heard anyone) say "I'm so much better than another"...because, of all of our different specialties. When talking about the Facebook incident with a few other brothers, they all agreed that it shouldn't have been so public. I'd just like to say that I'm a fan of transparency. Put it all out there! The Facebook incident started a larger conversation about Drew's approach to Twirlin'. No necessarily his skill, but his thought-to-be aggressive approach to getting brothers to Twirl with him. They've stated to me, on multiple occasions that they feel as though they've been slapped with a left hand glove and challenged! to a dual...LOL. I think that it stems from the elitist of elites culture in the community of *kanemasters*. When one is outcast or denied his warranted acclaim, he may feel like he has something to prove when in fact, he doesn't.

I talked with Drew extensively, and I'll be the first to state on paper (and the 1000th verbally) that anyone who can Twirl five canes, or one on his head and two in his hands while on a unicycle is a hell of a master. He knows how many hours he puts into each trick. He's a lot less crude than most of us who freestyle. To the defense of the *freestyle kings* (myself included) there is something that we've witnessed as pleasing to the crowds about cane improve. To sum it all up...Twirlin' needs everyone's representation, and I'm not sure that any one person can be called the best except when they're in the spot light.

The best reference might be 1999, where there was a significant style change from the Texas masters to those of Alabama. When the 10 year reign of smooth-steady-flow from brothers in TX met the speedsters and tricksters from AL, Mike Slider and Rod Moody both walked away from what is known as the *battle in the dirt* thinking that they had the superior showing. And so they did, depending on who was judging. My first huge challenge was in a roller skating rink outside of Birmingham, AL...and I was (in my opinion) out done by a younger brother named Santagio. He flipped in the air and tossed the cane up and caught it behind his back....and I caught myself in awe...LOL. I was staring just like everyone else. He told me at the end that I *killed it* referring to the freestyle that I did just after him. I'm sure that my facial expressions showed that I thought differently.

There are so many great stories of battles in Twirlin'. Having stated that, I was compelled to participate in this publication because it would be the first of its kind.

If I'm not mistaken we were in New York City in August of 2010. I was interviewing for the Harlem Book Fair. I met Kwesi in New York just before, to catch up on everything, and he suggested publishing a book about Twirlin for the conclave in 2011. Twirlin' just seemed like something we used to do. This was central to Kwesi's point. He thought we needed to record as many experiences as possible to set the stage for the next 100 years.

I myself wondered if the death of an artistic form like Twirlin' is a result of the shroud of secrecy and competition among a relatively (to the general population) secretive group: fraternity. When I was learning, brothers simply didn't want to share what they knew, because of their competitive culture. While watching other Twirlin' I've regularly heard, "Oh, he got his moves from that guy...or this guy", when it's necessary to acknowledge that we've all been inspire in some capacity by everyone else around us. None of us were self made, from the Texas step teams of the late 80's to the ASU Kream Team of the 00's.

Hearing that "Twirlin' is over" was discouraging to state the least, so Kwesi started taking some survey material from those of us who were judged by our peers as being superior in the craft for one reason or another. They all had different specialties and styles, but they are all known by some audience in the north, south, east , and west. Most of the feedback that Kwesi was getting confirmed what we heard: Twirlin' "is a dying art".

From a humanistic point of view, something as socially intuitive as getting together with friends to share a story, a drink, a little rhythm, was being lost. Far greater than Twirlers, or the Nupes, or African

Americans, the suggestion that humans are having trouble bonding and transferring skill sets the old fashioned way (one relationship at a time) is compelling enough to become a bit activist. Hopefully this text inspires some conversation, nostalgia, and meeting of the masses to do something that we do so well: interpret the beat and woo the crowd.

Hopefully Twirlin' isn't a dead art, and the YouTubers we all notice are just a reset. I'm looking forward to Twirlers sharing, what they've got, so that the next time someone is called a master it will be critiqued and know across the globe instead of a few back yards.

May 2011   James Felton Keith
Toronto, Ontario, Canada

Part One
The When

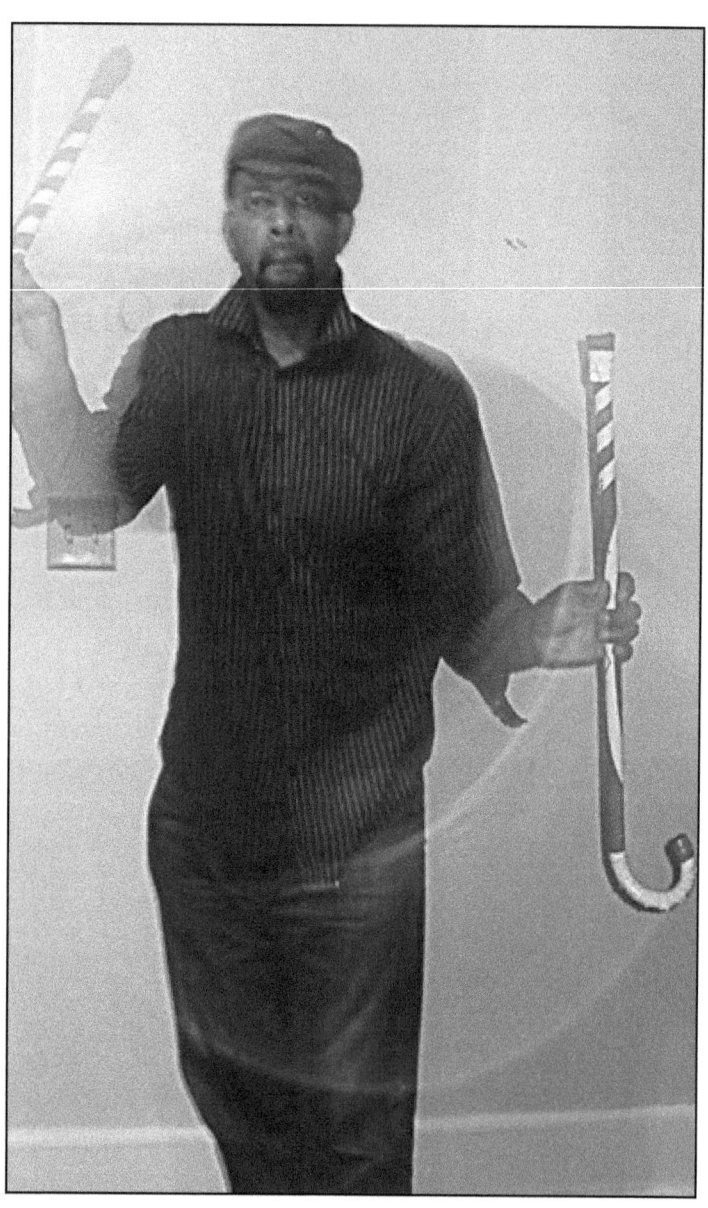

A brief history of the Cane

I've tried to condense a more ancient historical account of cane wearing that can be found in more relevant texts. While the culture that inspires cane twirling or what we now know as Twirlin', is necessary to understand this text is a brief history of a still fledgling art form that has yet to take its full form as formidable entertainment art in American and its spawn cultures.

Twirlin' is the art of cane twirling. It evolved out of stepping, a rhythmic performance involving moving one or more canes around the body with speed, accuracy, and showmanship and has been developed by members of black greek lettered organizations (BGLOs) since the 1940's; however, it is most associated with the members of Kappa Alpha Psi.

The development of Black Greek Letter Organizations' (BGLOs) step shows witnessed the emergence of what is affectionately titled Twirlin'. In order to understand the significance of Twirlin', one must first understand the history of the cane and how its use has evolved overtime.

The purpose of the cane has evolved over time from the pre-dynastic period through today. The name in addition to its purpose has evolved over time.

The cane was a symbol of protection, power, nobility, and gentility. The cane has been a part of human history since the pre-dynastic period. In Egypt, the cane was represented on hieroglyphs as a symbol of the pharaohs' nobility. One of the oldest canes ever found was located in a pre-dynastic grave in El Omari, Lower Egypt. The cane as a symbol of power, guardianship or prestige appears in both ancient and modern art and emblems.

Early shepherds utilized the cane as a staff to both corral sheep and defend against animal attacks. In the 17th, 18th, & 19th century Europe, it was regarded as symbol of gentility. Despite the titles-haqa, crook, staff, scepter, walking stick, or cane, and it is traditionally regarded as a symbol of authority for any individual possessing it.

Throughout history as cultures took on certain beliefs, the status of canes and staffs changed. In the early 1700's, the first settlers in America used the canes as a status of wealth and refinement. Over time, the Puritans passed laws which wouldn't allow extravagant dress or displays of wealth. This, in turn, altered the perception and appearance of the canes used.

In London England 1700's a gentleman had to procure licenses for the privilege of carrying canes. It was expected that they would abide by certain rules or risk loss of the privilege. However, believe this or not...it was really because of the etiquette police! It was considered an extreme violation of manners to carry a walking stick under one's arm or for that manner to brandish it in the air or to drag it on the ground or to lean on it while standing.

In reality, no matter where you look in history, you will find a staff or walking cane of some kind. Those that were to represent wealth and power would be made to show status. Those used for support or for recreation would be created with more simplicity.

During the course of time, the walking stick became a status symbol for men and woman all over the world. You only have to think of the bishop's staff and the scepters of kings and emperors that symbolized power.

BGLOS and particularly, members of Kappa Alpha Psi Fraternity Incorporated have always worn or carried canes since the beginning of the Fraternity in 1911. As we understand it unintentional in its inception, this occurrence soon became an unofficial tradition of theirs, as they've always strived to be noble and productive members of their community. The cane, being representative of gentlemanly status, it would have been ideal to exhibit such a characteristic.

This type of display became commonplace up until the 1950's when Black Greek Letter Organizations, on an undergraduate level, began to practice what are now known today as "Step Shows".

Undergraduate members of Kappa Alpha Psi Fraternity and Phi Beta Sigma Fraternity took part in the trade and soon incorporated the use of the cane, into the routine. This was something that spread throughout regions of fraternity life in the black culture during the 50's and 60's.

Stepping evolved at different rates on various campuses. In our account, Kappa Alpha Psi member Thomas Harville, who pledged at West Virginia State College, says that in 1940, his fraternity participated in group singing, often while they were holding hands or moving in a circle, but they did not step. As he told it "through the years brothers added singing and dancing, and in recent years we started using canes when we step. It was not until the mid to late 1960's that the undergrads of Kappa Alpha Psi Fraternity began to decorate the step canes with the colors of the organization. The usual design was to pattern the cane with one crimson and one cream stripe from tip to tip.

All throughout the 50's and 60's, canes used in the art of stepping were standard canes of approximately 36 inches in length, give or take half a foot. Members of Kappa Alpha Psi would perform routines know as "Taps" where the canes would be beaten on the ground in time with the rhythmic beat of the step show.

The turn of the decade would reveal an evolution in cane stepping known today as "twirling". Undergraduate members of Kappa Alpha Psi in the 70's, not content with Taps alone, would then create a new form of cane mastery which involved much more skill and talent than merely banging the cane on the ground to a certain beat.

During this time, members of Kappa Alpha Psi Fraternity, Inc. began to "twirl" canes. Now that "twirling" had become the new style of cane stepping among Kappa undergrads, members were constantly searching for better and faster styles. One problem that Kappa's faced during this time is that they were still practicing the step show routines using the standard sized, 3 foot canes. Kappa's widely found that while standard length canes worked fine for tapping, they became a hindrance when it came time to twirl. Thus, cane stepping evolved once again with the birth of the short cane.

Thus, the full length cane, as well as standing straight up in order to perform a "Tap", has been sacrificed, making way for agility and speed.

"During the last two decades of the 20th century and the beginning of the 21st century, step enthusiasts have been fortunate to see a variety of individuals and step entities emerge as twirlers or *Kanemasters* as they are more commonly known. There have been numerous names to emerge as legendary since the days of "Dirty Red" of Texas. The Twirlin' phenomenon has taken a following of its own aside from stepping or step-dancing. The Cane-masters hail from as far west as California through Nevada, Texas, Alabama, Mississippi, Arkansas, Tennessee, Illinois, Michigan, Indians, Georgia, Florida, North Carolina, Boston, and through New York.

The Twirlin' phenomenon has transformed itself into a digital art on the net, via websites like Facebook.com, Youtube.com, Myspace.com, and most recently Twirlin.info, a social community that caters directly to Twirlin' patrons.

The testimonials contained in the succeeding pages come from seasoned cane twirlers who have each demonstrated a commitment to developing their twirling skills to the highest levels. These master's of the cane and eternal students of the art. As you will learn, the time and commitment demanded of the cane in order to reach the highest levels within the art require an unrelenting dedication to becoming "one with the cane". These brothers are the history of Twirlin' and have honored these pages with the next chapters in the history of Twirlin'. You will learn about the role of the Twirlin' culture in Birmingham, Alabama in the development of superb cane masters around the country. Enjoy!

Part Two
The How

Twirlin' Dictionary

These are the known terms that can be identified as essential moves to have been collected by individuals twirlin' across the world today. Of course this is a growing list of terms and as Twirlin pervades local cultures, it will take on new forms and naturally names.

2nd count revolution

- The user will rotate the cane 720 degrees through all '4' fingers stopping at the thumb at which time the hook of the cane will point to downward (6 o'clock).

  This method is most common; however, there have been derivatives of this method preformed where the cane ends its revolutions at 3, 12, or 9 o'clock.

  (Typically thought to be the most primitive form of Twirlin')

1st count revolution

- The user will rotate a cane 360 degrees while trading the cane from right hand to left hand at the end of each revolution, creating the illusion of a continuous revolution.

Windmill

- The use will rotate the cane 360 degrees from its CG [center of gravity] while passing the cane from right hand to left hand creating the illusion of a continuous revolution.

Body wrap

- The user will cross both hands around any limb to pass the cane from one hand to another making the creating the illusion of the cane wrapping around a specific limb or group of limbs.

Kane Master

- An individual who has mastered the Art of Twirlin' from a mechanical standpoint to reap acclaim from peers and admirers.

    Masters are never self proclaimed

Freestyle

- An unrehearsed compilation of moves, twirls, and tricks.

Series

- A group of rehearsed moves spanning some period of time.

Bopp

- A step used by Steppers to keep time and uniform during a cane series or step show; however, twirlers elaborate on Bops to cater to a specific snare (drum) count or unsounded rhythm.

Catch

- The user will toss a cane into the air at a timed rate to make a catch with an arranged limb. Catches have a wide range of complexities and revolutions.

Break

- The user will stop the normal momentum of a cane after a revolution to direct it in the opposite direction and finish the move in/on the newly directed area/limb.

Illusion

- The user will use a particular move or series of moved to elude the mechanics of a more complex or virtually unattainable move.

Trick

- The user will use move the cane in such a way that actual revolutions are not encompassed into the move. A Trick could be specific to a limb, body type, gender, or setting/prop.

Kick

- The user will use a foot to direct or toss a cane to a pre determined position, limb, or prop.

Of course there are some moves within Twirlin' that are more intuitive...the kinds of moves that allow for anyone to make a seemingly seamless transition from one Trick or Bopp to the next. We like to call these the Diamond Foundation, or four must haves.

2nd Count Revolutions

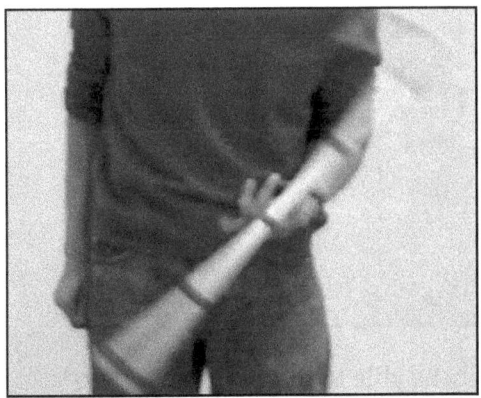

Starting with the hook pointed downward, it is necessary for any uniformed show, to be able to Twirl the cane over each finger and create a continuous revolution using the thumb to guide the cane in place.

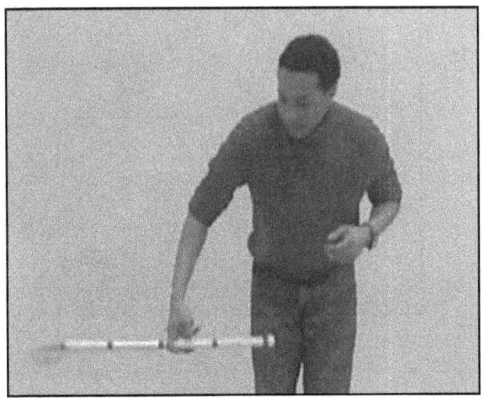

When using the 2nd count revolution parallel to the ground, it is important to slightly pull the cane up while moving the cane through each finger. It's an illusion, as gravity won't permit any continuous Twirlin parallel to the ground.

A master should ideally be able to twirl the cane in a 2nd count revolution at every direction possible.

1st Count Revolutions

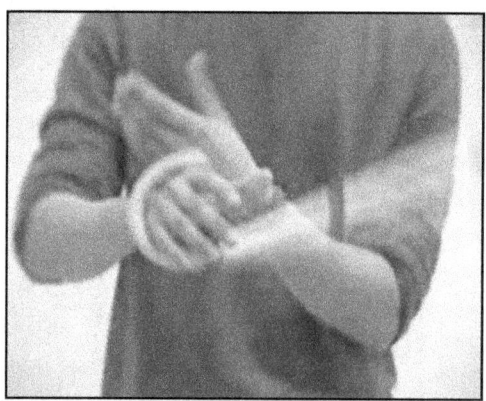

In our experience we've seen most beginners attempt a 1st count revolution using their wrist. While there is no *wrong* way to Twirl, we think that there it's a poor way to control the cane. The arm is simply too long to control the movement of the cane. We recommend the space between the thumb and the index finger only.

This will allow anyone Twirlin to manage the cane in multiple directions. The ease of opening and closing the hand allows for maximum control just in case of a potential DROP!, and those are never acceptable...LOL

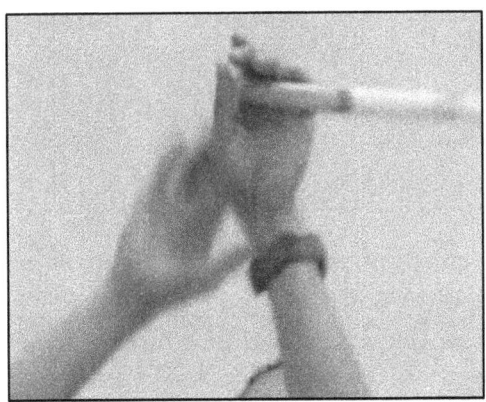

Windmills

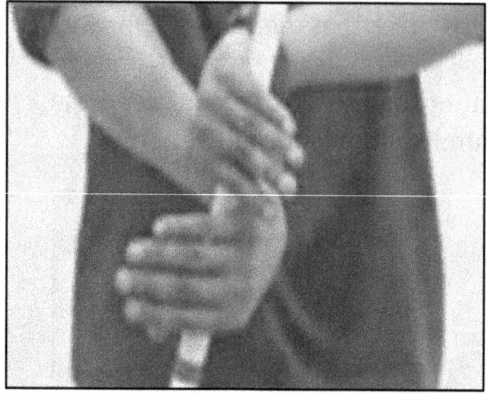

To be clear, there is nothing intuitive about the windmill, but once the mechanics of the move are understood it should be relatively simple to plan and execute a move with a windmill.

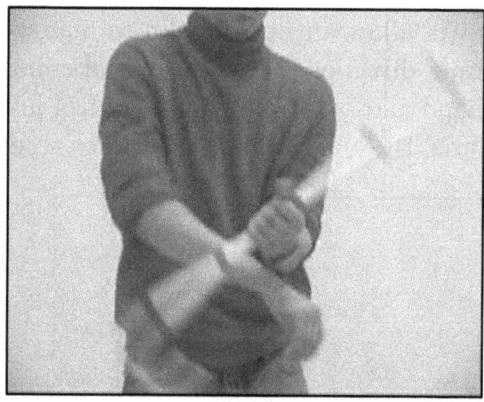

While it looks like a constant revolution, it is actually two separate 306 degree revolutions from the right and then the left hand→ In that sequence. Of course it is impossible for the wrist to turn 360 degrees (unless something is wrong).

The ideal windmill is executed by holding the cane with the right hand facing thumb down. Hook placement doesn't matter (it could be pointing up or down). Note: it is always necessary to consider the weight of the hook, as it will make the flow much more manageable.

With the right hand, rotate clockwise ~270 degrees, or until ability is exhausted. Then drop the cane into the left hand. Catch in the left hand with thumb pointing up. Then rotate the cane in hand clockwise another ~270 degrees, or until ability exhausts, to catch in the right hand at the original (thumb down) position.
→Repeat→

Body Wrapping

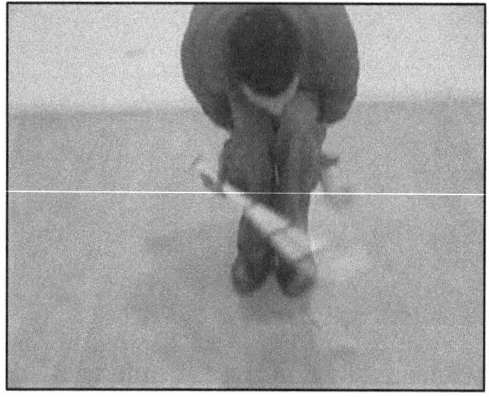

Wrapping should be the most simple of our four move diamond foundation.

As the picture illustrate, anyone Twirlin should cross their arms (in an 'X') and pass the cane from one hand to the other.

The placement of the hook is irrelevant. The placement of the catch is equally as irrelevant. Body wrapping is not specific to the waist, let, and neck. Consider it a wrap anytime the arms are crossed and the cane is passed from one hand to another. We've seen people wrap behind their back, and even under-the-leg and over-the-back....These should not be confused with the "one handed body wrap", as that move doesn't use two arms or the specified cross.

Part Three

The Who

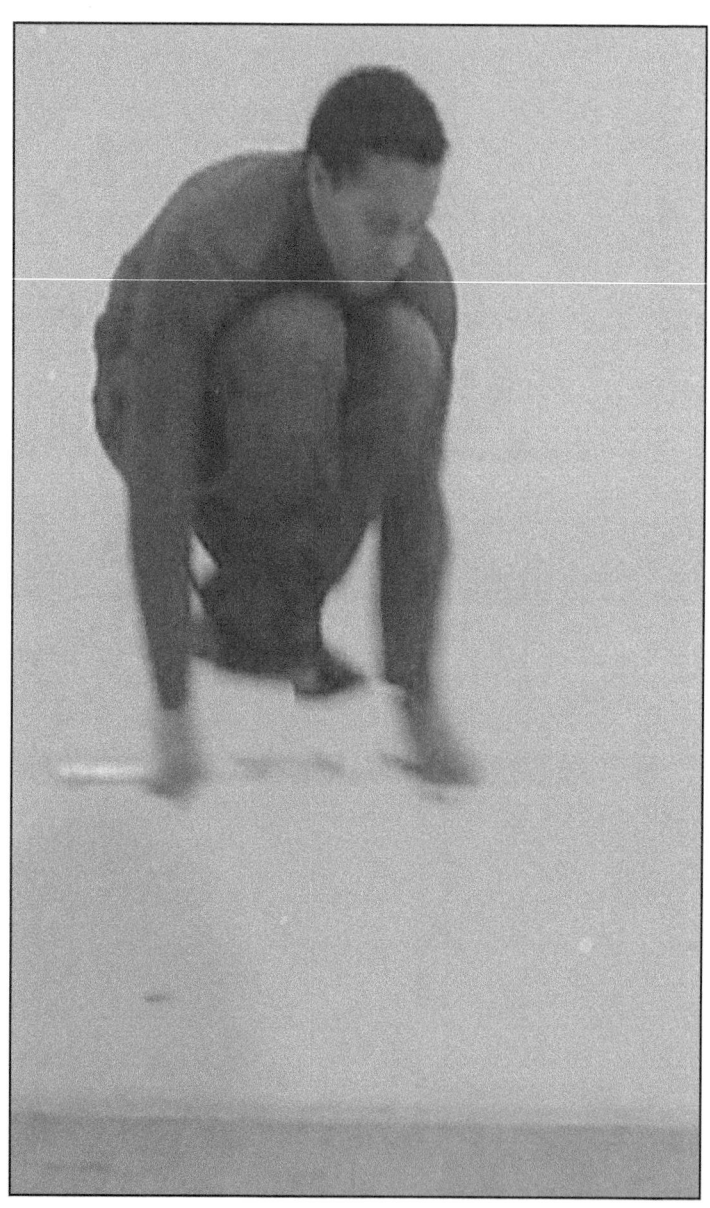

Interviews

To give every Twirlin' enthusiast out there an ideal of what, how, when, where, some of the best of our best got, view, and remember Twirlin' as an art form we took the following interviews from Kanemasters that you may not know so well...in their own words.

We've done our best <u>not</u> to modify the integrity of how these testimonies have been given to us. We've kept the format and language true to their original delivery. Feel free to L O L .

.

With some help I've managed to ask the following.

- ❖ What year did you start Twirlin'?
- ❖ What made you start Twirlin'?
    - o Who inspired you (if anyone)
    - o What inspired you (if anything)
- ❖ What factors (if any) helped in your development of the skill set?
- ❖ When was the first time that you realized you had a superior skill set in comparison to others?
- ❖ What was the biggest stage or best performance that you recall giving?
    - o What feelings/emotions can your remember?
    - o What reaction did you receive from the crowd?
- ❖ Is there a certain type of cane or style that you'd regard as superior or more attractive?
    - o If so, please do explain
    - o If not, do you regard all Twirlin' as attractive, please do explain
- ❖ Do you have a philosophy about what great cane Twirlin' is?
    - o If so, please do explain
- ❖ Where do you see the skill set in the near and far future? (Please be honest)?
- ❖ We'd love to read any other details about your experience that you feel are misunderstood or require greater clarification.

The responses that we received were lively to state the least. In random order these Kanemasters will take us all on a journey through their time of development.

D-Fin

My name is Damian Findlay and I represent the Gamma Epsilon Chapter of Kappa Alpha Psi. I can remember it just like it was yesterday. It was April of 1997. I was a neophyte fresh of the sands and hungry to enjoy the new life birthed in me through Kappa Alpha Psi. On a hot April day at the home of "Eagle", we were fraternizing with beer, liquor, chicken and fish as usual. A NUPE named Fred Fleming and a NUPE named Ricky Punch were exhibiting their kane skills on the back patio. My eyes sat in amazement at the level of skill and acrobatics these brothers displayed with confidence, poise, and smoothness. It was like Sade's track "Smooth Operator" came to life. Come to find out that both of the aforementioned brothers were well known kanemasters. I salivated with every second of the kane spinning. I went to ask both of these brothers to teach me. They both agreed, but told me that it took them years to get to level of skill that they had. I was a little discouraged at first as I was a novice that could barely twirl the cane through his fingers. However, I was determined to become adept with the kane. That summer 2 of my line brothers, Alvin King and Bryant Waller, worked with me to teach me the basics. Once I saw that I had the basics, my determination increased. Later on that summer, Ricky and Fred saw me twirling. Both of them told me that I improved drastically and that one day I would be "tight with the kane". This was the impetus for my determination to become a kanemaster.

I studied these brothers diligently and I soaked up everything I could from them whenever they were around. My confidence level increased with the kane as I began to "get loose" at parties with people complimenting me and telling me that my kane skills were "ill." At this stage in the game, I was a Rick Punch/Fred Fleming hybrid. Little did I know, my own creativity would start to be birthed. I started to develop my own style which I would call finesse on fast forward(aka smooth speed). My creativity blossomed and the NUPES on the yard told me that I went from the worst to the "COLDEST"

My ego grew, but it would soon be humbled(lol). Picture it Homecoming 1998. A NUPE named Rod "Zorro" Moody was in town. This brother's style was intimidating as he had speed, precision, and FUNK. This brother ate my alive at a K A Psi houseparty (while still wearing his sportcoat might I add). I went hard and lost bad. Little did I know that this guy from Birmingham, Alabama was from a city that breeded twirlers the way Big Boi from Outkast breeds pitbulls. The interesting thing though was after I lost, he told me in his ever so Birmingham drawl "NUPE you goin be fire with that kane. I sense your hunger". We kept in touched, twirled together often, and became the best of friends.

I took my twirling on another level. I knew that I had arrived when one half of the Theta Delta dynamic duo called Batman/Robin challenged me to a twirl off at a GE houseparty in front of a lot of people. I was a little intimidated at first as this guy was one of Birmingham's finest and he was taunting at me while generating a crowd of honeys and bruhs. However, GE was hyping me up big time and I was on that

YINE(Wild Irish Rose)----Great combination. Little did I know, tonight would be the turning point in my life. He lost-------BADLY. I was in a zone where twirling spirit takes over the body and you're pulling off 20% moves. The more the crowd cheered, the more I ate his ass up(LOL).

Not too long after that, Rod Moody invited me to go to Tennessee with him to challenge some guys in Tennessee that claimed they were the best. They too lost badly. After this session, Rod Moody actually referred to me as a kanemaster. I couldn't believe it. Zorro, the guy that beat "Dirty Red" called me a kanemaster. This is when I realized that I had taken twirling to an exemplary level.

What more can I say? I could go on for hours about trips to Kappa Luau, Kappa Beach party, Memphis, Boston, stepshows in Birmingham and Atlanta University Center, and being filmed in Rasheeda's "Walk like a soldier video".

If I had to speak of the most memorable moment I had it would be at the 2001 Theta Delta "Bare As You Dare". Rod Moody and I were in a zone. I was doing things with the kane that were beyond my imagination. Even my drops were getting "oohs and ahhs". Old school NUPES were comparing Rod and I to Andy Ragley, Sean Day, and Ricky Punch. At this point, I "owned" the fact that I was a kanemaster.

Over the years, God blessed me to come in contact (in some form or fashion) with greats such as:

1. Ricky Punch,

2. Fred Flemming,

3. Rod Moody,

4. Johnny Edwards,

5. Dave Jefferson,

6. Kenny O' Rourke,

7. Devin McKnight, Pieface, Boyd----shout out to Gamma Sigma

8. Dirty Red

9. Sean Day

10. Eric Thomas

11. Travis Gooden

12. James Keith

13. Paco from BZ

14. Talmedge Stevens

15. Carlos Mclain

16. Nick "Chilly" from Tennessee

17. Jason from Theta Delta

18. Patrick "P smoove" Smith

19. Santiago, Jamal, and Eric Branch for Eta Chi

20. Ronnie Braxton

21. Andy Ragley

22. Lee Toliver

23 Bryan Banks

24. Stanley Turner

25. Eric Hughes

26. Bobby from IT

If there are any greats that I came in contact with that I forgot, please forgive me for not paying you homage.

These kanemasters showed determination, perseverance, humility, and PASSION. These are the qualities that make a good master. Of all the aforementioned qualities, passion is the most important. Being a kanemaster is like being in a brotherhood with a brotherhood. It is a badge of distinction given to those who have exemplified mastery of the kane after years of diligent practice. There are many drops and bruises on the road to becoming a kanemaster. Many aspirants to the kanemaster association fall by the wayside due to a lack of determination and mental fortitude.

Unfortunately, the art of twirling seems to be dying. The hunger for the art seems to have fizzled out(it's on life support if you will). I pray that at the centennial that a renaissance of twirlers will rise out of the midst like the last avatar.

David K Boyd

1. What year did you start Twirlin'?
   I started twirling in fall of 2003.
2. What made you start Twirlin'?
   a. Ronnie B (NU Rho Fa 99) and Jamacus Turner (AD Spr 02) otherwise known as JT.
   b. Before I was a member of Kappa Alpha Psi I saw a step show with Ronnie and JT do an all Twirlin' show. My home chapter (AD) is not very popular with stepping in shows but more of Twirlin. I have never seen a show with all twirls before or knew it ever existed. That is when I got inspired.
3. What factors (if any) helped in your development of the skill set?
   My chapter created an environment that the smoothness of Twirlin is better than its tricks. It looks better when someone can make a one hand body wrap not look like a trick but more of its regular pattern.
4. When was the first time that you realized you had a superior skill set in comparison to others?
   When I put my first video on YouTube I was compared to my DP which is JT. He was much smoother than I when it comes to completing moves.
5. What was the biggest stage or best performance that you recall giving?
   a. The best performance was stepping with Denver Alumni in 2008. It was a great performance because we controlled the crowd. Even when we had our mistakes

in the beginning, we made up for it at the end.
    b. Our reaction was the best at the end. Traditionally Kappa step shows always have a scene for the ladies. That was our last step before our outro. The great part was the audio guy actually delayed our music on accident for the outro in which worked out perfectly because it gave the crowd the chance to scream. We ended with a standing ovation.
6. Is there a certain type of cane or style that you'd regard as superior or more attractive?
    a. I think that smooth Twirlin looks better on stage that tricks. Tricks tend to break up the flow of the show. Not to disregard tricks but if the performer can make the tough moves look easy and the easy moves look tough, he has mastered the skill.
7. Do you have a philosophy about what great cane Twirlin' is?
    a. Great cane Twirlin is creating your own style and figuring out what looks good to a crowd. Knowing how to enable tricks without making it look difficult. Being made in the south gave me a new outlook on what Twirlin is supposed to look like. Twirlin is an expression of individuality in Kappa. The great twirlers in Kappa (James Keith, Paco, Red, Ronnie B, and E. Branch) all have their own styles but all know how to

control the crowd. They know which moves work, they know which ones they do not try on stage because it risky of a drop.

8. Where do you see the skill set in the near and far future? (Please be honest)?

    Now that I am tenured in Kappa (7 years) I know how to move a crowd in my home town of Denver, Colorado. I am considered the best in the state. In Nashville it is a humbling experience. I come from a Twirlin chapter so two of my line brothers and my DP are better twirlers than me. Also Nashville has other chapters with great twilers (AT, Nu Rho, Eta Gamma etc.) So my skill set out of 10 is a 7.

9. We'd love to read any other details about your experience that you feel are misunderstood or require greater clarification.

    I was the first to twirl on youtube. I know I am not the best twirler but I can say I started a revolution. Truthfully I didn't know what youtube was until I saw someone saved me on myspace and they *youtubed* themselves playing the piano. I'm glad I can be a part of history.

Kenny O'Rourke

1. **What year did you start Twirlin'?**

   1989

   2. **What made you start Twirlin'?**
      a. **Who inspired you (if anyone)**

      Todd Armelin (Alpha Sigma Spring '88), Dirty Red (KN), Yogi(ZB), Big Huck(KN), Myron(KN), E Hughes(B upsilon), ZORRO (HX), Fitzgerald (BI), Silky Slim (A Sig), Carlos McClain (DT), Talmadge (DT), Suave Bob, B Blanks (B Tau), Shevy (GK), Rashidi Barnett (GK), Geoff King (LD), John Frank (LD), Fred (BO), D Fin (GE), Pat Smith (Pi).

      b. **What inspired you (if anything)**

      The moves initially, then my friends started Twirlin' in Kappa League. I hopped on the bandwagon in 1990.

   3. **What factors (if any) helped in your development of the skill set?**

   Listening to the ones who came before me, showing humility and deference to them and watching old skool tapes.

   4. **When was the first time that you realized you had a superior skill set in comparison to others?**

Freshmen year in college in my interest group, THE ROLLIN' 60's.

5. **What was the biggest stage or best performance that you recall giving?**
   a. **What feelings/emotions can your remember?**

   Labor Day Weekend Classic Step Show @ CAU in 2000.
   b. **What reaction did you receive from the crowd?**

   Let's just say my stock went up. LOL

6. **Is there a certain type of cane or style that you'd regard as superior or more attractive?**
   a. **If so, please do explain**
   b. **If not, do you regard all Twirlin' as attractive, please do explain**

   I respect all forms of Twirlin' as long as a brother has his own style and swagger. I am a combo of Southeastern, Southern & Southwestern styles because all of my Twirlin' brethren are from those provinces.

7. **Do you have a philosophy about what great cane Twirlin' is?**
   a. **If so, please do explain**

To me, cane Twirlin' is another way for a bruh to present his personality without even talking to you. You can tell a lot about a brother by the way he twirls.

8. **Where do you see the skill set in the near and far future? (Please be honest)?**

    Unfortunately, I see it as a lost art. With the exception of a few, nobody is really getting in that "PIT" and battling. Back in the day, it was an honor to be the tightest twirler in the province. Now, Bruhs just keep that cane in their back pockets for show.

9. **We'd love to read any other details about your experience that you feel are misunderstood or require greater clarification.**

    Again, I respect all forms of Twirlin', but I really respect the ones that get out there and showcase their skills. To you young Bruhs, don't be afraid...get out there and represent like we used to do.

Drew Brown

WHAT YEAR DID YOU START TWIRLIN'?

I started Twirlin' in the Fall of 1993.

WHAT MADE YOU START TWIRLIN'? WHO INSPIRED YOU (IF ANYONE)? WHAT INSPIRED YOU (IF ANYTHING)?

My father took me to a stepshow in the DC area. Most of the step teams were Omegas, but there was one team that used canes. I recall asking my father about them because they were unique. Later, in collage at Kansas U, I noticed two things when the Nupes entered the room that day. 1. The room fell silent (with respect). 2. The Nupes all walked and interacted as though connected by a (magical) Bond. During that time period "Xavier" (Beta Iota) had great show. They were able to simply travel and win shows whereever. They won the show at Kansas U. and Mu Chapter also performed. I was impressed by the show, but I still left not knowing the name "Kappa Alpha Psi" or even that there was a significant difference between Kappas and Sigmas.

As the Fall semester came, I knew that I wanted to join a fraternity, but I did not know which one. My only exposure to Greek life was Omega (via my father), School Daze and Revenge of the Nerds! I went to the informational meetings for Sigma, Omega, Kappa, and Alpha. I even considered predominantly white fraternities. I spent hours weighing the pros and cons for each organization. I considered everything from being an Omega legacy to what color my white socks would be if I accidently washed them with fraternity colors! I called my sister (a Delta) for advice. Still, I had no strong passion one way or another.

One night, I decided to meditate until I could make a decision. I laid in bed thinking for over an hour. Eventually, I started to give up, relax, and go to sleep. Just then, it seemed like my eyelids filled with a cloudy glowing crimson light . . . and then I saw a vision of a crimson cane floating towards me! At that moment, I knew I wanted to be a Nupe.

The sole cane had personal significance. I immediately called a Mu Chapter Nupe and exclaimed that I was absolutely sure I wanted to become a Kappa. The cane itself inspired me to twirl, and in part, to become a Kappa. Of course, I had a dozen other reasons too. My ships and I taught ourselves to twirl in a couple of stolen moments. Unlike most of the well-known kane masters, I did not have the benefit of Kappa League, or video tapes or the Internet. Back then, to get taught (trademark) tricks by older Brothers, one had to be considered "a Nupe" and continue doing community service (as to not be considered a "t-shirt wearer").

Later, I was also inspired by Mu Chapter's legacy. I feel extremely lucky to be a Mu Chapter initiate. For one thing, during that time period, Mu won "Chapter of the Year" awards for at least a decade.

Attention to detail regarding tradition and proper protocol was also paramount. Being a member of a single letter chapter has benefits, but it also has "costs." The legacy of Mu Chapter includes Kappa luminary Dr. Oba B. White (who was also a Mu charter member), Gale Eugene Sayers (NFL great), Wilton Norman "Wilt" Chamberlain, and Reuben A.

Shelton, Esq. (currently on the Grand Board) among others. This rich legacy is no small feat considering the extremely low number of Mu Chapter initiates. Mu Chapter members are pioneers. I craft my cane style in part, as an interpretive expression of Mu Chapter's pioneering legacy. In fact, my stage name "Maniac Drew" comes directly from "Maniac Drew" and the describes my maniacal performance style.

WHAT FACTORS (IF ANY) HELPED IN YOUR DEVELOPMENT OF THE SKILL SET?

Mu Zeta. It is rumored that the Mu Zeta chapter (Southeast Missouri State U.) chapter took a hiatus from school in the Fall '93 just to haze. The hazing death came the following semester which led to the 2-year Kappa-wide moratorium on intake. During that time, I moved to the Atlanta area. Unable to form a step team, I decided to do 1-man step shows (at step shows where there was no Kappa representation). To date, I have never practiced or performed with a traditional step team. Being a "1-man show" has been the basis of my cane freestyle development. I took a 6 year break from the cane (from 1998 through 2004). Then, on a whim I got obsessed with extreme off-road unicycling and that led me to join the Texas Juggling Society. There, I focusing on learning new (and very difficult) cane freestyle tricks and techniques.

WHEN WAS THE FIRST TIME THAT YOU REALIZED YOU HAD A SUPERIOR SKILL SET IN COMPARISON TO OTHERS?

My very first show was at an HBCU where I technically won first place. At the time, I didn't have an aim to be better than other cane enthusiasts. In fact, I realized that I had very little exposure to cane culture and even less natural talent. I did things like twirl in the dark to fast paced music to get better. Most of what I know I taught myself (and had to "create" it). In the beginning, I just wanted to do dropless performances and represent Kappa (in the absense of a Kappa team). I was eager to teach and learn from others and simply enjoyed drinking and twirling. In later years, I specifically focused on technically difficult tricks (2 - 10 canes). Lately, I have been focusing on 1 and 2 canes (but I still haven't found a strong passion for 1 cane). Recently, I saw the depth of what can be learned on 2 canes (i.e. club swinging, poi spinning).

WHAT WAS THE BIGGEST STAGE OR BEST PERFORMANCE THAT YOU RECALL GIVING? WHAT FEELINGS/EMOTIONS CAN YOUR REMEMBER? WHAT REACTION DID YOU RECEIVE FROM THE CROWD?

Since crowd reaction varies, I tend to perform for myself first, then the audience. For example, Clark Atlanta's Homecoming in 1997. It was a dropless show, but I didn't pick popular music or play to the crowd.
For the finale, I lit a cane on fire. As soon as blindfolded myself with my sock, I heard an Omega shout "If he hits me with that cane, I'm going to jump on stage . . . " Other Omegas chimed in as well. I could also hear the Deltas (seeming to grumble in fear) and screams from AKAs. I could also hear the Sigmas and Zetas to my left. They seemed happy. Overall, the audience felt apprehensive. In that moment, I could smell everything from the perfume of audience members to the burning fuel of my cane. As I worked the three canes blindfolded, I could feel the air current in the room and the heat of the fire as it surrounded my body. For a moment, it felt like I had "flow" and it was though I was tumbling through space. I still perform hoping to experience more personal moments like that one . . . but I don't really remember the final crowd response.

Another show that I recall was on a road trip to North Carolina A&T.

The Alpha Nu chapter there sang lots of songs. There was about a hundred Nupes in a circle and then at least another hundred ladies forming an outter ring. Eventually, we got to Zoom Golly! I got to do the last chant, and then for a show, we played "Drop Cane" (where Brothers perform until they drop). Guessing that I had the most skill, I went last . . . but I quickly ran out of tricks that I could do in a not-so-sober state. With that, I yelled "I need some Hype!" and the crowd automatically responded "You got the Hype!" and then I threw the cane high into the air. As I looked up, I saw my cane appear to be about toothpick sized. I had thrown it "too high". Then, to my dismay, the cane started drifting backward . . . with the wind. I started running backward hard enough to pull one of my leg muscles. I closed my eyes and leaped high into the air like a frisbee dog. My catching hand was behind my back. As I fell into the audience behind me, it seemed as though a Brother had lightly put a cane in my hand. I pulled the cane from behind my back, and to my surprise, it was my cane! The crowd and I jumped with excitement.

IS THERE A CERTAIN TYPE OF CANE THAT YOU'D REGARD AS SUPERIOR OR MORE ATTRACTIVE?

I've spent a couple thousand hours practicing juggling 5 canes. When juggled, wood canes last 100 - 200 hours. After a while, I realized that making and maintaining canes was taking 30+ hours per year. To solve that problem, I designed a new cane that is cheaper to make, more durable (depending on the stress), much lighter, and that does not require tape. I also modeled the hook to be larger to match my first/best cane and large ankle size. The new (plastic) canes are far less intimidating to new users. I find more people willing to experiment with them than wood. Overall, the new design is superior to the traditional wood setup so I have been using them almost exclusively them for years.

IS THERE A CERTAIN STYLE THAT YOU'D REGARD AS SUPERIOR OR MORE ATTRACTIVE? IF SO, PLEASE DO EXPLAIN. IF NOT, DO YOU REGARD ALL TWIRLIN' AS ATTRACTIVE, PLEASE DO EXPLAIN

I created a style I named "cane freestyle". Cane freestyle is defined as "the freedom & ability to move canes with diverse styles & techniques". The art includes cane Twirlin' but also includes juggling, balancing, spinning, and all types of movement. Artists are free and have the power to ignore the cliche' cane twirling conventions. However, with "great power comes great responsibility".
Cane freestyle artists are compelled to learn and perform a wide variety of styles and techniques. After all, one is not "free" to do "cane freestyle" if they lack the freedom/ability to perform a major technique (like juggling).

Prop arts (like baton twirling, cane Twirlin', toss juggling, nunchuck twirling, contact juggling, poi spinning, etc) are generally confined to exclusive styles of performance. For example, baton twirlers have set standards as to "what is cool" and they generally dismiss most of what toss juggling has to offer. Likewise, toss jugglers generally don't do many common baton twirling tricks or techniques. All of the prop communities are segregated from each other and there is very little overlap. The current culture stifles communication. Even worse, some prop artists look down on other prop artists because their prop (and it's culture) defines what they think is good art.

Cane movement (as an artform or sport) is far less developed than baton twirling or toss juggling (where there are rules, conventions, Worldwide competitions and formal judges). There is a brief opportunity to define "what is cool" with regard to canes. I'm hoping as "diversity". There is a wealth of knowledge in the various prop communities to exchange. Fortunately, skilled baton twirlers, toss jugglers, and spinners, et al. are to able to perform their styles and techniques with canes. Therefore, the cane is the best suited to be "the universal prop" and the cane paves a path to creating an ultimate prop artform. Cane freestyle offers both the artists and the spectators far more variety.

DO YOU HAVE A PHILOSOPHY ABOUT WHAT GREAT CANE TWIRLIN' IS? IF SO, PLEASE DO EXPLAIN.

To a large extent, "great cane Twirlin'" mirrors average baton twirling. Mechanically, it should have at least a dozen different tricks, transitions that double as tricks, very little (or no) repetition and should be fast sections. For the most part, it should be smooth. Watch any competition level baton twirler for an illustration. Granted, there are lots of things canes can do that batons can't, however, there are lots of things baton twirlers are doing that cane twirlers aren't. Imagine 12 year old baton champion Stacy Singer in a cane Twirlin' battle.

WHERE DO YOU SEE THE SKILL SET IN THE NEAR AND FAR FUTURE? (PLEASE BE HONEST)?

I believe cane twirling will expand into cane freestyle. I hope to inspire cane artists to go to the next level. For the last few years, I have been traveling the country filming hundreds of performers from all over the World using canes. Each performance contains different styles, tricks, and techniques. The video will be released for free and I have plans to make sure it gets more visibility than all of the current cane videos combined. Pressure for improvement will either come from the artists themselves (in the spirit of competition) or from the spectators begging the question "Can you do that?" Moreover, the video will show what is possible with canes and bring many "fantasy tricks" to reality.

Another aspect of cane freestyle is found in the variety of venues. I've casually worked on "performing on all stages". Like other cane artists, I've won step shows and cane battles. However, I was also filmed for a music video (Love You Down, INOJ), movies (Stomp the Yard, Hulu), done numerous parades and community service events, auditioned for America's Got Talent (2011) and even performed cane freestyle as a job. To date, I've been to at least 10 conventions related to cane freestyle. I have even pitched a tent and went to a special camp just to study 2 cane movement. I am the first 1-man show to be officially supported by IHQ; I performed at the 2009 Conclave as a solo, and was financially compensated.

I'm working on paving the way to a full-time cane freestyle career. From what I have seen of performance artists, there is definitely room for a career in cane freestyle. With a polished cane freestyle act, there are many organizations that will fly you around the World so that you can perform. I'm not as confident making that claim regarding cane or even baton Twirlin', but if you can twirl AND juggle AND spin, you should always be able to find work. To make up for a deficit in natural talent, I have practiced thousands of hours. I used to walk 7 - 10 miles a day practicing 3 to 5 canes. On

Juneteeth 2010, I performed (solo) in a parade for some miles, juggled at the park for World Juggling Day, and did my 3 hour practice. The next day, I noticed my shoulder (permanently) separated. Now, when I do cane freestyle, the pain accumulates and stays for days. I've been to numerous doctors appointments and I'm currently considering surgery. I believe that one day, there will be a cane freestyle artist that has the skills of all of the top artists combined. They will probably need to start practicing at 6 - 12 years old (like other performance artists). I realize that I started too late to be "The One" for cane freestyle, but I am working towards being "Morpheus". I am the pioneer, the future talent will be the polish.

Much of what is slowing the evolution of cane Twirlin' (and cane freestyle) is secrecy. Chances are, your favorite "kane master" is suppressing video footage. For some, protecting a personal legacy trumps adherence to the fundamental concepts of our Bond. Generally, the individual tricks and techniques being suppressed can be copied relatively quickly. The video I'm working will doubles as "an encyclopedia of cane skills" and there will be plenty of material to learn. On the other hand, many of the tricks in the video take years of practice to perform. If you see a trick in the video that you like, it's free. Copy it . . . if you can. The point is cane Twirlin' (and cane freestyle) will evolve in the direction of the information that is shared (rather than suppressed). The video is called "co-cane". For more information (and updates on the project) visit canefreestyle.com .

Paco Veela

1. **What year did you start Twirling'?** 1995 (Deltric V. Latham a.k.a. Paco Veela) 2k1-B.Z.Kanemaster 57-0

2. **What made you start Twirling'?** It's funny. Round 95, during my freshman high school life, twirling was a religion in Birmingham. Everyone that was live knew how to twirl. So, one day, standing outside our band room at Ensley High, three members of A-Psi (a popular high school frat) was standing in a circle passing the cane around. I was fascinated. The girls were looking amazed and interested. So, I continued to look on and all of a sudden, Frank (one of my homies) passed me the cane, in an effort to make a mockery of me. I was hesitant at first but I eventually gave in. Understanding that I had never twirled before, I began fumbling with it. To the amusement of all the guys and girls, I looked foolish. That moment stuck with me a long time. I used it to fuel my drive to become the best twirler in Birmingham. About 8 months later, during senior week, Frank and his frat brother were preparing for a show in the auditorium. I happened to be outside while they were basically killing time twirling. Just my luck, I had been practicing everyday. Frank tossed me the cane. To his astonishment, I proceeded to kill him his frat brothers, in front of everybody. My skills were raw and fast, really fast. People looking from the windows began clapping for me. He never asked me to twirl with him again. I took it as a compliment.

a. **Who inspired you:** An assortment of twirlers influenced my hunger and my style of twirling. The following: William Metlock, David Jefferson, Charles Keenan, Adrian Story, D-Fend, Ali, Dirty Red, Andy Raglin and a majorette name Kanisha.

b. **What inspired you (if anything):** Honestly, the fame inspired me. Birmingham loved twirlers. They worshiped them. They were always known as the livest of the live. The one person that could go out on stage, amaze the crowd and recruit fans for the frat. It was a performers' mentality and I wanted that responsibility. I wanted to feel invincible. I wanted to be the best. The livest and most renowned twirler ever.

3. **What factors (if any) helped in your development of the skill set?** Well, my skill set is derivative of fundamental twirling skills. For instance; left and right hand fluidity, an assortment of body wraps, leg tricks, wrist tricks, neck tricks and the mastering balance.

4. **When was the first time that you realized you had a superior skill set in comparison to others?** The first time I realized this was in 1996. My first show at Talladega College. I was a member of Kappa League and we drove down (on a school

night) to perform for their Kappa Week. I was so excited. Anyway, we arrived at the step show early. The crowd was still filtering in and the bruh's were just standing around twirling. While this was going on, Darryl, one of my Kappa League bruh's, was twirling. A few of the Nupes were looking at him with a sarcastic smirk on their faces, so our president (Clavion Goldsmith) whispered to me two words: Get em'! So, I did. I freestyle battled against almost 15 Nupes before the show began and I killed each one of them in front of the crowd. I was 13 at the time. After we performed, I began walking to meet my fellow leaguers, then a tall, thick, college woman aggressively approached me and said," I wanna Freak you like you freak that cane." I was terrified. In that moment, I realized the power of twirling and how mature my skills were becoming.

5. **What was the biggest stage or best performance that you recall giving?** I have performed a lot. I mean, almost everywhere. I have been performing since I was 13. I have done at least 61 shows collectively. Furthermore, as a freestyler, one of my favorite performances happened during the Greek picnic 07. As a team, my favorite show would be a toss up between 106 and park 2008 (when we won) and a Tuskegee show that we performed at in 2004. During that Tuskegee show, the crowd's applause literally made the walls quiver. It was classic. We performed with only four guys and they turned the music off on us during the crème session. After a heated argument on stage, we defied the authority and continued with our

show. The Crowd went bananas and so did the bruh's. We lost the step show but we won the hearts of the entire crowd. A show that we did in Detroit was just as monumental though..

- a. **What feelings/emotions can your remember?** When I'm free styling, I always get a butterfly feeling right before I twirl, but when I begin, it's like my cane calms me and we begin to create art together.

- b. **What reaction did you receive from the crowd?** Every time I perform, the crowd reception is always appreciated. But there have been times when it's been overwhelming. I can vividly remember times where crowds of ladies have rushed the dressing rooms in search of us. I can recall, during a performance that we did with PLIES, he called us back out on stage to stroll and I dived in the crowd. That was the first time that I have ever been carried by an enormously large group of women. Fantastic.

6. **Is there a certain type of cane or style that you'd regard as superior or more attractive?** I prefer light, slender, slight long canes. Kane's of that caliber allows your twirl to look better and your tricks usually coincide with it.

    a. If so, please do explain: Light canes are more maneuverable to me. I hate heavy canes. They are only meant for pledging or fighting q-dogs. Light canes are easier on the wrist and helps increase speed and longevity in twirling sessions.

    b. If not, do you regard all Twirlin' as attractive, please do explain: Honestly, I use to be very critical of twirler, but now, realizing that its almost an forgotten art, I take pleasure in seeing even the most novice twirl.

7. **Do you have a philosophy about what great cane Twirlin' is?** Yes.

    a. If so, please do explain: Great cane twirling is a dedication all by itself. It involves diligence and unrelenting practice. I've put knots on my head, bloodied my lip, broken windows, dented cars, hit girls (in the crowd) and felt that it was all worth it. I even went an entire summer twirling with my left hand so that it would catch up to my right hand. To be great is never easy, but the rewards are benevolent.

8. **Where do you see the skill set in the near and far future? (Please be honest)?** Do to

the vast information and recording technology that is available now, I think that legends like James and me have really affected the skill set of most beginners. I frequently see twirlers that have borrowed bits or pieces of our twirling styles and combined them with their own. I don't mind because I want the twirling movement to carry on and flourish. However, it always amuses me when a lower level twirler attempts to battle me using moves from either James or myself. I always ask," where did you learn that," the response is always, "YouTube." I then begin to laugh and recognize how many people actually look at us as the leaders of this twirling revolution. I have envisioned that there will be a dude, from a small school, with an unknown name, that will succeed us.

9. **We'd love to read any other details about your experience that you feel are misunderstood or require greater clarification.**
The only factor that I would like to express is the movement and revolution of strolling. Strolling has been a popular asset to any chapter since Brian "black" Barker (BZ 2k3), Derrick "Dmoe" Moore and myself began creating a different but effective strolling style in 2003. Since that time, we have created, recorded and performed our style of strolling. Our style of shoulder rolling has engulfed the old technique and renewed itself. In proof, if you see any tapes of bruh's strolling before us in

2003, it different and simple. We transformed it into a symbol sex appeal and Nupe swag. Now, every chapter strolls and rolls their shoulders like us. We are the founders of the upgraded shimmy swag.

Zorro

My name is Roderick Moody, BKA Zorro the Province Killer and I am a Student of the kane. All those that consider themselves Masters are merely marionettes when they wield the wood, subject to its whim. This is the first and easiest riddle of the cane: Submission. The kane has many riddles though, and during my career I have been fortunate enough to solve a few.

I grew up in Birmingham, Alabama, a veritable monastery of kaning style and culture. In 1993, I met my first and most influential teacher there; He could take an all white kane and transform it into a blinding white circle when he twirled. This teacher was the epitome of style and tricks and taught me moves that I still use to this day. Just like Chinese Martial Arts, there are many styles within the kaning discipline, but like the majority of Birmingham kaners I focused on speed and tricks, practicing and practicing until I could execute my moves flawlessly.

As a graphic artist, the aesthetic of my art form is of great concern and importance to me. After I built a kaning foundation, I began to find myself studying and critiquing the mechanics of my style. I examined my hands and arm placement during tricks, how I stood, and what angle would the "crowd" see my moves from and more. This water shedding, which took place over the course of several years, was paramount in the development of my ongoing kaning presentation.

My true baptism into the art form took place at Konklave '99. I'd emerged from my meditation cave, a stronger twirler with a cache of innumerable tricks, impeccable timing and devastating combos that not only helped me remember my tricks but maximized them as well. I'd also joined a chapter with a seasoned Birmingham kaner Johnny Edwards (HX), whose experience and tutelage were priceless. I was the consummate Southern Province twirler at this point, all tricks and speed, and in my mind, unbeatable. To make a long story short, I showcased and battled many at Konklave that year but nothing compared to the memorable "Battle in the Dirt" vs Dirty Red and the Southwest Province (which is how I got my nickname, by the way). That battle is legendary for many reasons, but it's most meaningful to me for reasons that significantly vary, I'm sure:

#1 I got to meet and befriend a true Student of Kaning, Dirty Red (KN) that I still talk to and admire to this day

#2 It was the first time I witnessed a style other than the Southern Province's

#3 I think it was the most obvious Change of an Era in Kaning ever.

Initially, admittedly I didn't like the SW Province style and thought it was simple, but after Dirty Red lent me his tapes, I began to appreciate it and see the complexity in it. It was also a very lyrical style. I was told that they practiced to Jazz, while we practiced to the latest Hip Hop music. There were many differences, too numerous to list, but together these styles were indomitable and with the help of Dirty Red, Eric Hughes and other dedicated Kaners we were able to completely integrate these styles which is one of my proudest achievements.

I think balance is the key to being a great Kaner. I don't think most Kaners take into account the art of the form though. I used to worry about levels; put it in the air here, kneel there, then bodywrap. You must keep the viewer's attention otherwise to the uninitiated; it becomes boring or seems repetitive. I don't see enough timing tricks nowadays, which was one thing I specialized in. The art of Multiple kanes has all but disappeared to my knowledge and it seems that to be a good kaner with only one is sufficient, which is sad. At the end of my studies, I was proficient in 1-6 Kanes, could compete and win a stepshow on my own or lead a step team. I studied in every aspect of the art form and always pushed myself.

One thing I've noticed nowadays, especially when young kaners speak to me (when they can find me, lol) is that they set out to be Kane Masters, I set out to master the kane; Therein lies the difference.

Kwesi "Preditor" Daniels

1. What year did you start Twirlin'?

   2002

2. What made you start Twirlin'?
   a. Who inspired you (if anyone)-

   The cane masters at Gamma Epsilon (Tuskegee University), specifically my ship James.

   b. What inspired you (if anything)-

   I was always amazed at how the Kappa brothers manipulated the cane through their fingers and around their bodies effortlessly- I thought it was easy until I picked up my first cane.

3. What factors (if any) helped in your development of the skill set?

   My catalyst for developing the skill set was my first step show. I practiced for the show every day, to ensure I would not drop. I knew I needed to be comfortable twirling in front of people, so I practiced twirling moves as I commuted on the bus, train, and walking. I challenged myself to be able to twirl while standing on the platform waiting for the train, without dropping the cane one the tracks (I couldn't get it back if it fell). I did everything I could, to ensure, I would not be overly anxious in front of a crowd. As a result of my preparation, I performed a solo and heard my first roar of the crowd. I never put the can down after that!

4. When was the first time that you realized you had a superior skill set in comparison to others?

> The art of twirling is developed through twirling battles. I realized I had developed a superior skill in comparison to others when a Nupe I battled the previous night called me up and congratulated me on beating him. This was big for me because Nupes don't admit defeat!
>
> What was the biggest stage or best performance that you recall giving?
>
> One of my biggest performances was twirling in Detroit during a Kappa Cruise with my ship James. James had recently been voted best twirler in the nation and I developed my skills by battling him. This was one of my most memorable performances because it was the first time I had ever twirled with him in his home town of Detroit. We traveled up and down the three levels of the ship doing impromptu performances wowing the crowd. We shut the party down at each level. Our performance were so exceptional and jaw dropping, no other Kappas stepped onto the floor to battle us.
>
> > a. What feelings/emotions can your remember?

I was overwhelmed with feelings of achievement. It was one of the first times I twirled in public with my ship and the first time I realized I had developed the skill set to perform on the same stage with him.

    b. What reaction did you receive from the crowd?

The crowd went crazy when we came on the floor and started twirling. The DJ put the spot light on us and started mixing the music to our performance. The crowd was in awe at what we were doing with the cane. We left the cruise with the respect of the brothers and the gleaming admiration of the women. Many approached afterward to congratulate us.

5. Is there a certain type of cane or style that you'd regard as superior or more attractive?
    a. If so, please do explain
    b. If not, do you regard all Twirlin' as attractive, please do explain

I believe it is all about the flow and NOT DROPPING! Many beginning twirlers focus on the tricks and are unable to twirl continuously. If you only have tricks and no flow, I don't respect your skill. I believe anyone can learn tricks, but it takes a lot of practice to perform tricks within a flow. The most unattractive Twirlin' is DROPPING! Don't do it! Never perform moves you are not comfortable performing in public. The first time you drop, you lose the respect of the crowd.

6. Do you have a philosophy about what great cane Twirlin' is?

    a. If so, please do explain

My philosophy about great cane Twirlin' is to be able to make the most difficult moves look ridiculously easy.

7. Where do you see the skill set in the near and far future? (Please be honest)?

As I have traveled the country, I've noticed it is more developed in certain regions over other regions. As Twirlin' becomes more mainstream, I see the skill set becoming more developed by neos and younger brothers in regions outside of the traditionally dominate regions like the South and Southeast.

8. We'd love to read any other details about your experience that you feel are misunderstood or require greater clarification.

Twirlin' is an artform that is developed around the fundamentals. All new twirler's should spend relentless amounts of time working on the fundamentals. All great twirler's and Twirlin' moves spawn from the fundamentals.

Johnny Blaze

1. What year did you start Twirlin'?

    I began twirling at the age of 15 (1992) after I attended my first step show. I remember seeing the NUPE's on stage and being amazed at how these guys were able to dance with the cane. It was "magical".

2. What made you start Twirlin'?
    a. Who inspired you (if anyone)
        i. I was inspired by both the NUPE's in my city (Birmingham, AL) and guys in the high school frats who would always have their canes with them in the mall and in parking lots. I remember being young and seeing these guys just doing amazing things with that piece of wood. It was art.
    b. What inspired you (if anything)
        i. I was inspired by the challenge to be connected to the art form. I wanted to create something new and be part of a movement that was really big at my time in Birmingham, AL.
3. What factors (if any) helped in your development of the skill set?
    a. The competition during the early 90's really influenced me. There were so many good twirlers during my teenage years. People were twirling in high

school in preparation for college. We had high school fraternities that did nothing but step. In many ways, the high school groups were better than the NUPE's because of the amount of time that they had on their hands to practice. I remember that I would see groups of guys in alleyways in different neighborhoods practicing. It was a very common sight in the early to mid 90's in Birmingham, AL.

4. When was the first time that you realized you had a superior skill set in comparison to others?

    a. The first time I realized that I was good was when I was recognized by my peers. It's something that you cannot claim, it's something that others must claim for you. You had to be known, you had to be revered, someone had to use something that you created. Once you start to see your style being emulated by others and people coming up and speaking to you about teaching them or how they saw you, then you realize that you were on that level. That's when you become a master.

5. What was the biggest stage or best performance that you recall giving?

I can't really say I can point out one stage. I was in 33 shows. Many of those shows were significant for different reasons. They represented different times in my life, different stages in my development as a twirler, and most importantly, the various relationships that I built with my step teams. I most of these shows, I was the cane master. I usually had to teach a lot of my team from the ground up. I made a connection with each and every one of those guys. Getting on stage is not only a test for yourself as a master, but for the people that you brought up, the guys that are under you. They represent you. If they fail, you fail as both a team and an individual. I remember spending hours on end with each individual on my step teams. We would watch tapes together, analyze how they would catch a pass in a particular position, how a twirl wasn't going through fast enough to transition into the next move. We would sit down and work out solutions for their particular issues. As a cane master, you understand that no one performs the same show. Yes, we are all on the same stage, performing together to the same song and the same routine, however, we all have different responsibilities. As a cane master, you have to be totally connected to your group and understand where the pressure is being transferred. Everyone has a point in the show where they will be challenged and it comes at different times. The cane master has to be able to know who is thinking what and when it's happening. He has to be able to look out for hoes in the formation before they happen, he has to make sure that people are not zoning out or getting too tired. He has to be aware of dropped canes, mistakes that happen behind him, misplaced props, etc.

All of these factors play into to each and every show. Every time I walked off the stage, no matter how we placed, I always was satisfied, yet I wanted to improve. There was no ultimate show or best performance. I only dropped three times in 33 shows. Those three shows I was very disappointed, however, I learned from them and grew as a performer.

As far as crowd reaction is concerned, it varied. As I grew older, I became wiser and learned how to prepare for a show. I always visited the campus before I made up a show, walked the campus, watched my potential audience, walked the stage and the arena, etc. I was very very detail oriented. I left nothing for chance or assumption. My shows were catered to the crowd, I knew what they wanted and I gave it to them by the boat load. I realized how important theme's, costumes, props, team member appearance, etc was. I remember always joking about needing to pledge a white boy for the step team. I was ask another guy to grow dreads, and another one to work out and get really buff. I had a Drake on the team as well for the ladies and then the dark skinned shaven brother. It was all for the crowd. Heck, I even wished we had a midget for the crowd. I wanted to throw them every emotion possible. I remember coming from Birmingham in the early to mid 90's and being in a high school fraternity.

There was a lot of gang violence back then and we would always joke about someone getting shot and killed so we could dedicate a show to them and have their picture on the back drop, and that was at the age of 16 or 17. We were well aware of emotions and crowd reaction. It was built into us being raised as performers.

    a. What feelings/emotions can your remember?
    b. What reaction did you receive from the crowd?
6. Is there a certain type of cane or style that you'd regard as superior or more attractive?

I don't really regard a particular style as "superior" per say, however, I believe that you have to be able to be versatile to be considered a cane master. If the only thing that you can do is twirl with your right had or with 3 canes or juggle, then you won't get respect in my book. When I meet someone who I hear is a "master" I expect them to have the "known" art mastered... at least 80% anyway. There will always be that 20% that you don't know, which allows battles to take place. You battle over that 20% void. Who can fill it in the best? Sure I can go around my neck or catch the cane under my leg, but can you do "this"? That's what the battle was about. It was about challenging a master to push the envelope. It was about showcasing your "new" moves, moves that we were not taught, moves that were not part of the "system". Those were your signature moves that made you who you were and allowed people to put you above everyone else. A lot of twirlers these days consider themselves masters because they can twirl really well, however, 98% of their moves are these "system" moves that I can trace genetically to someone else. If you don't bring something new to the table then don't waste your time or mine. I didn't come out here to "share" my art with you and you're still dipping your pen in the paint. I remember watching guys twirl for 2 minutes and then I would ask them, "So when are you going to start?" Those are warm up moves that we do in step practice, I'm waiting on a trick, I'm waiting on something new. Going fast isn't a trick, it isn't special, it's not moving the art forward. Watching a video or taking someone else's difficult move isn't moving the art forward, and if you battle me, I will call you out on it.

    a. If so, please do explain
    b. If not, do you regard all Twirlin' as attractive, please do explain
7. Do you have a philosophy about what great cane Twirlin' is?

Great cane Twirlin is about control and innovation. Like I said earlier, a master must innovate to be considered a master. He also must have total control of his wood at all times. The cane needs to take on a mind of it's own, it's like salsa or tango and the cane is your partner.

    a. If so, please do explain
8. Where do you see the skill set in the near and far future? (Please be honest)?

I see the internet being the new battle ground for showcasing skills, which is both a positive and negative thing. It's positive because it brings people together and allows people to share their skills with each other whom normally wouldn't have the opportunity to meet. However, it also dilutes caning in several ways. Firstly, it detaches associations. In my days, the only way you could acquire a new style was to either create it yourself, travel to an existing style's origin, or meet a master who has traveled to where you were so he could teach it to you. This allowed you to sit down with them and work out for however long you had a chance to. At the end of the meeting, you two made a bond with each other. It was true brotherhood. You knew his style, he knew yours, you had respect for each other and all was good with the world. Also, if you ever saw his moves, you knew them intimately because they were taught to you by him. It was a very genetic way of being able to trace your roots, and also see where things came from.

James, when I first watched your videos, the FIRST thing I asked was, did this dude pledge in Alabama? He reminds me of myself and my boy Travis. I know that Travis didn't show you everything, but it is evident that you and him were close at one time and maybe showed each other some moves. That's what I miss about that close connection that we had as masters. It was a small group and everyone had their own signature style that was easy to trace.

Another negative is the lack of real life battles, which is making everyone studio twirlers. There's a big difference between a guy going off for 1 minute on a video that was probably shot 6 times until he got it right, and him doing the same thing with perfect timing on stage, with the crowd screaming, your hands sweating, and all the hot lights on you. Or at a party after you've consumed a little too much alcohol and a NUPE from another chapter challenges you at 2:00 AM and you're tossed into the fire with 100 people watching and you don't have time to prepare. You can't worry about if you're wearing a shirt that's too big or not tucked in or if you have on the high tops and can't pull off that ankle trick, or if your pants are too baggy or tight fitting. All those things matter. Being thrust into the unknown is what gave flavor to the battles. Having to perform anywhere at a moment's notice was challenging and scary. You never wanted to get dirt on your name so you had to step up to the plate. I remember back in the Spring of 1997, I had a horrible flu and had been throwing up for two days straight. The Alabama Statewide Step Show was that weekend and I wasn't even able to practice two days before the show. My brothers had to carry me around on their back because I was too weak. They were contemplating pulling out of Alabama Statewide because I was so physically drained. I lost 10 pounds of fluid and I never went to the doctor because I didn't have insurance at the time. I told them that the show had to go on and that I would perform. By the time the show rolled around, I hadn't eaten in two days, I was weak, sweating, and dizzy. They had to come get me and bring me to the arena to perform. I remember being taken around the back to the dressing rooms and hearing the roar of the crowd. I walked into the dressing room and remember the look of fear on my brother's eyes. I had a 9 man step team including myself, 9 girls that were part of the show and a 10 member crew for props. Out of all of those people, only 3 had prior experience on stage and Alabama Statewide in 1997 was really big. There were over 3000 people there that night. I got up in front of them and said, "I'm back, let's do this," and remember how the sigh of relief fell upon the faces of my team. On the inside, I was feeling like crap, but I couldn't let them know. I couldn't let my team feel less than 100% confident that I was going to be there and do what needed to be done. We went out there and had an amazing show. When it was all over, I collapsed in the back and they had to bring me water and some food. I tried to eat the food and I threw up some more. Then my current nemesis, a brother from Epsilon Epsilon by the name of David walked in. David pledged Spring 97 and was a beast with the wood. I had heard that he wanted me badly and was looking for a way to make his mark. He was fresh off the sands and was already killing people left and right. He challenged me right then and there. I remember some of my sands saying that I was sick and that it wasn't the right time. I stood up and said that excuses were tools of the incompetent. He started to spin and I stopped him and told him, if we are going to do this, let's do it outside in front of the crowd. He agreed and we left the dressing room and went onto the floor of the arena. It was in between acts and all the organizations were doing their thing, strutting and chanting and what not. Because of my deference he went first (a rule in a cane challenge). As he started twirling, the guys and girls from the other organizations stopped what they were doing and started watching us. I remember a crowd on the floor starting to encircle as and within 30 seconds, I was in the middle of probably 300 people watching David and waiting to see what my response would be. I remember that I could barely stand, but when he dropped, I just remember taking a breath, closing my eyes, and just going in. I remember people saying, he's not even looking, he's not even looking, but it was really because I was just too weak. We ended up going back and forth for about 10 minutes. At the end of the battle, he got me on a head spin trick which he had perfectly mastered and I got him on a soul-glow "I have the power Leroy" arm spin move that can still kill anyone to this day. It was a draw. He got his recognition and I kept my respect. After that, he and I became really cool. David went on to challenge the man that I handed my cane down to... Rodrick Moody... although some people may know him as Zorro, the providence killer. Him and Zorro battled for years and always ended in ties as well, although both claimed victory. David was a true master, adversary and a brother. And that's what you can not duplicate on youtube.

I believe that as we move further into the 21st century, we're going to continue to see new styles emerge as well as old styles disappear. I have not been too impressed with the rate of which change is occurring in the caning ranks these days. I do not feel like people are pushing the envelope the way that they were 20 years ago when I was coming up. There is not too much that's new and it's been a while since someone has wow'ed me with a trick. With technology these days, I am not sure if the art form will ever regain its' former shine. People are too busy these days to worry about caning. It's an art form that takes a lot of time and dedication to perfect and craft into your own. When I was in high school and college I didn't have the distractions that cats these days have. When I went off to the park to practice, I didn't have a laptop or cell phone or an ipad at my disposal. Nobody could contact me when I was in the zone. I was in my own world, just me and my wood. I went to a few step practices recently just to watch and people were constantly being distracted, going to their cars to make calls, texting their girl friends, even watching youtube on their phones. If you don't focus, then you'll never be able to get to that zone where it's just you and your cane. That takes an individual separating himself from society's worries and just being one with his craft. It only takes a few people to ascend to this level, however, I feel like I haven't seen this yet.

9. We'd love to read any other details about your experience that you feel are misunderstood or require greater clarification.

SNOTY The First

1. What year did you start Twirlin'?

> I started Twirlin' in 2001. I was a sophomore in college. My name varies among those who know me. Felton to most, James to few, JK to fewer, and SNOTY had a life of his own. It stood for Sweetest Nupe On The Yard, but I've been off the yard for a while now...LOL Keep the name change the 'O'.

2. What made you start Twirlin'?
    a. Who inspired you (if anyone)?
    b. What inspired you (if anything)?

> When I was in high school I joined the Kappa League in Michigan (Southfield Alumni Chapter), and I knew that the brothers used canes in step shows, but I'd never seen one. I could hardly spell Kappa when I joined. I thought it started with a 'C'...LOL. We were strictly a service and social group. But when I got to undergrad, and I saw the Nupes at Tuskegee I was infinitely intrigued. Two brother in-particular stood out: Michael Nelson and Carlos Smith. They would Twirl on the yard seemingly every day during the fall of 1999. I think that I was intrigued by the style and the mystery. I had no idea where to even get cane, or if I should. In the dorms a fellow freshman showed me how to Twirl with a cane he owned. He later became an Alpha, and we're friends to this day, so I won't say his name. There was always a bit of a buzz

around Twirlin' in my dorm, because everyone knew which frat I wanted to join from the first day I stepped on campus. I was type-casted....LOL

Of course, there were so many other people that influenced me along the way. Some of them were Kappas, and some of them weren't. One of the strongest influences was a good friend at a neighboring school, Auburn University of Montgomery (AUM). Cory Jackson was the smoothest. We had a bunch of mutual friends that he grew up with and I went to school with. I didn't realize that there was a Twirlin' specific culture in Alabama until he showed me what the Huntsville style was, and the Texas style , and of course the Birmingham style. They were all variation of tricks, slow rhythmic Twirlin', and speed. Everyone had their pick of what was the best. It usually depended on where they were from. I still remember being at AUM and asking the Kappas who their cane master was, and those that were honest would say "Corey". There were a few that would actually get together over his house to Twirl, on the hush-hush to get their skill up. I would just watch in awe.

Around the same time my other influences were from Birmingham, Alabama. Travis Gooden, one of my oldest friends from undergrad. He had been Twirlin' since high school and made sure that I could Twirl in every direction with either hand. He said "if you can't do this man, there is no need in acting like you can Twirl". According to the Nupes, he taught most of them that came before him to Twirl. He was like the 21 year old historian living off of campus telling stories of the "old days" as if he were 81 and pioneered the art. He knew everyone and had most of the good stuff on VHS tape. We watch Twirlin' from the late 1980s up until the late 1990s. He showed me what some of the cultural differences were between the Alabama Twirlers and the Texas Twirlers and everyone else. Down south there were only two places that really produced masters and those were Texas and Alabama. Nowhere else really mattered to them. And per what I saw, nowhere else really should have at that time. Travis and I would Twirl and talk about the day when we'd make it over and do a show with the Nupes and exactly how we would do it.

In 2001 another generation of Kappas were crossing and I was standing on the sideline watching, along with Travis, and it was devastating to see everyone else showing out and Twirlin'. I can remember traveling to AUM to Twirl with my next influences. They had no classes on Friday, so we'd skip ours and travel up there on Thursday night to *kick it*, that was the slang. We'd all get together at Cory's house. He still wasn't a

Nupe, but the Nupes called him the Kanemaster when anyone asked in that particular setting. The real beneficiary of the Thursday night Twirlin' session was D Fin. He was a Nupe, and was hands down one of the greatest to ever do it. He was a hard core trickster. He would let us Twirl' and then go do tricks we inspired in public...LOL....it's all hilarious now, but I just wanted to be out there back then.

Of course, there were lots of Nupes and others that I encountered who influenced me to some degree but the five mentioned were by far the most influential. And then there was number six: Paco. In 2001 the Beta Zeta neophytes came from Alabama State to do a show on the Tuskegee yard, and Travis and I watch from far away, a bit jealous and knowing that we had something to show the crowd. I had no idea who the brothers coming from Alabama State were, but Travis pointed one of them out. He said (talking about Paco) "you see that one, he is going to kill this show". Paco was the first person I saw that was able to combine all of the smoothness from Texas and Huntsville, and the speed from Birmingham with tricks. After that show I petitioned the school to get my own dorm room, so that I could practice: 106 Emory 4. The room was all white, and I had a white refrigerator. By the end of the Fall in 2001 (about eight months), that place was spotted black like a Dalmatian form the black rubber stopper on the end of the first cane I bought from Wal-Mart. I'd just go back to the dorm at Tuskegee after studying and partying and watch the videos from Travis. I can't remember if he gave them to me or if I took them...LOL The videos were from a Kappa Conclave in 1999 with Dirty Red of (KN) and Zorro (HX) and Franz Hughes (BU), there were a couple of others, but I never got to know them personally but their legends were as wide spread as Red and Zorro. I tried to do everything they did in the 1990s, and put my own spin on it. I think I was a pretty decent Twirler by 2002 but I hide it to avoid being singled out by the Nupes.

3. What factors (if any) helped in your development of the skill set?

By the end of 2002 I was traveling to other states with my friends and the Nupes and taking a cane of course, and most people didn't know who I was until I was there. The inevitable battle between chapters and frats is what made me better. My ships and chapter brothers were always saying that "if we go somewhere and you get beat by anyone, it's going to be hell". It was the constant "Challenge!!!". My first challenge was May 11th, 2002. I remember it because it was the day before graduation and Travis was graduating. He couldn't be the chapter Kanemaster from somewhere else. So we hit it, and I did a few new moves that I had been working on (they are all old now...LOL), and won the brothers approval, even though Trav would have said he went easy one me...LOL.

Then there were the street battles; my ship Ced "BigKnasty" Keeton and I used to hit in New Orleans. He would hustle Nupes on Bourbon Street. He would challenge then, and bet money, and build their confidence, even though he is a much better Twirler than most of the people I've seen in the past ten years. After the Nupes bought in to Twirlin' for Ced's price, I'd come in on cleanup crew. It was classic. At one point they pulled us into a club on Bourbon Street (Bourbon Street Blues Company). The crowd grew quick, I think they thought we were some break dancers or something like that. They started chanting "Get on the Stage, Cane Boy","Twirl". Ced, Nick "Japan" Mack, and I were like a traveling Band during Mardi Gras, Essence Festival, and Bayou Classic, every year for a few years.

The New Orleans stuff was a given, but I think I got significantly better in Tuscaloosa at HX. There is a younger brother Santagio (Spring 03' if I'm not mistaken). He was a killer. His tricks were made for crowds. They were what I used to call, jaw droppers. I remember Twirlin' at a skating rink. I can't remember which city, but I was *ate up* by this younger brother from HX. My chapter brothers never let me hear the end of it. Santagio and Ialways remained friends and we did a show in 2007 at the Conclave in Minneapolis/St.Paul. We made that show up in 30 minutes at the most in the parking lot of Paco, Santagio, and Mike's hotel...LOL. It was classic. I don't think that any of us were in school, but we found one of the Alumni Chapter advisors for the HX and Gama Phi chapters to sponsor a team. Paco came up with the name Kanemasters Association and we said we were all SP. We won a check and it went to those chapters. The show was great even though I dropped (I had a horrible cane after mine broke backstage). The real show was the night before. We took canes in the club that night. I swear we were literally Twirlin' on top of every bar, with the crowds chanting, we were on table tops. Santagio was hanging from the balcony, Mike had a crowd that backed him into the bar, Paco got on top what looked like a stage, but it was elevated and there was a circle of women around it. It was like Live.

4. When was the first time that you realized you had a superior skill set in comparison to others?

My first Conclave 2003 in Charlotte, NC.
I thought I was good, but I was sure that there were plenty of other brothers like me. I knew about Paco and Santagio, but no one else who was our age and likely to show up to Twirl. But again, I was sure that there was someone. Apparently they all skipped that Conclave.

Franz Hughes took over the step show and told the crowd of some +5000 patrons that we were going to have an exhibition of an "ancient art"...to suggest that no one really Twirled canes anymore. I was with my chapter brothers and the brother from Epsilon Psi (Sp, 99'), and we were hyped up, all neos, all strollin' around the room...kick it! So Franz called a circle to pick three brothers to go on stage and Twirl for the crowd. I walked to the back of the auditorium to talk to the Nupes form the Northern Province Alpha Beta (Sp. 01') chapter while the group narrowed. I was honestly terrified that I would start Twirlin' and everyone would blow me away, and that was the reason I wanted to go last. After Franz had picked three, I ran up to Twirl just for a few seconds, and he said "you are in, and you (pointing at someone else) are out, let's go on stage".

When we got on stage, the crowd looked like a sea of people. I didn't do stages. If I remember it correctly I went second, but it could have been third. The whole time the first brother was on stage Twirlin' I was in the shadow of the DJ Booth Twirlin', heart racing, thinking about falling off the edge. The first Nupe dropped after a really good flow, the crowd applauded, and he exited. I think I Twirled with that brother in 05' in St. Louis, but I can't remember his name for the life of me. I think 03' was the first time any of us had been on a stage with that many people looking on. It was standing room only. The Nupe that was the DJ asked me "what song do you want to hear". I was probably as red as my shirt like "dude, play whatever, I don't care", I do remember saying that.

I walked out on that stage and the music dropped, and it was that song by 50 Cent and Lil' Kim, "Magic Stick". It was big at the time. All I know is I heard "I got the magic stick", and the crowd started going crazy, it was the best high. As I started to Twirl, it got comfortable like being at the frat house with Ced and Kwesi....and I was not dropping at all. The crowd went so crazy. I think they were all standing up chanting "I got the magic stick", but that could have just been my memory. Now I'm sure I went second, because the last Nupe to Twirl dropped and the crowd started yelling "encore, encore". All I remember is Franz saying "your new name is The Coldest", and the rest was loud music and cheers all around....hahahaha. At the end the Nupes started throwing 100 dollar bills from the DJ booth, They were taking bets. I was a broke college student, then looking back out at the crowd it seemed that they were all women wearing sorority shorts. Needless to say, the rest of the weekend just got exponentially better.... (evil) LOL.

5. What was the biggest stage or best performance that you recall giving?

a. What feelings/emotions can you remember?
b. What reaction did you receive from the crowd?

I've actually been on a lot of big stages since the conclave show in 2003. Since that time, I Twirled for a large crowd at every conclave, including St. Louis, Minneapolis, and Washington D.C....and so many other shows at chapters and schools wherever I've traveled. I even did a Twirlin' exhibition at University of Witwatersrand in South Africa after a basketball game. The Minneapolis/St. Paul show was a special show because four of the best from the Southern Province got together and created a show in 30 minutes at the hotel parking lot. It was Paco from BZ, myself, Santagio from HX, and Mike from GPhi. I dropped the cane on stage, which hadn't happened until that point in 2007, but the show was Epic from a Twirlin' standpoint. Just to be a bit redundant and juvenile about it, my cane broke backstage during a practice and I used this POS (piece of shit) on stage. The whole time I was out there I just wanted to walk off, but that would have been worse.

The biggest, grandest stage I can recall is YouTube.com. It changed my life as it changed the world. By the time YouTube.com came about I'd graduated from college and was trying to get away from the college life. But we can't just walk away from the past. I happened to be visiting my girlfriend and she lived near Kwesi Daniels and his wife. When I walked into his office, he showed me David K Boyd's video on YouTube, and said "we have to do this now". LOL...but he was an architecture professor and still on the clock. Later that day we met at his new house and his wife agreed to let us tear up the walls before she picked colors for that room. Clearly some differences from how we used to kick it and Twirl...LOL. We cut those videos "Nupe Twirling" and "Nupe Twirlin 2" that night in January 2006. I think David's came out in January and ours came out in February. I'd gone back to business school a little after that, and for a course project in entrepreneurship I made some videos with brothers from Delta Pi (what up CP from DP) chapter to sell. There was a real demand for those DVDs, so I built a website and marketed the product and ran distribution out of my girlfriends house. She was packin and slangin em' while at that time I move d out of the country to China and then South Africa for work, those DVDs moved like drugs. After a while we just posted them on YouTube for free, it became a hassle to manage, and so many people wanted to learn using those DVDs just as I had learned from watching Dirty Red battle Zorro in VHS tape... LOL Capitalism corrupts.

6. Is there a certain type of cane or style that you'd regard as superior or more attractive?
    a. If so, please do explain

    b. If not, do you regard all Twirlin' as attractive, please do explain

I'm a fan of it all. I love seeing the tricks that look like they hurt, that I will never attempt to do after hitting myself in the face hundreds of times back in 2001. I also love seeing that Twirlers that can just flow for hours, making it look like the cane is one continuously moving entity. I've always tried to create what most of us who Twirl call flow. It's a mindless type of freestyle that just comes from knowing yourself and what you can and can't (just as important) do.

7. Do you have a philosophy about what great cane Twirlin' is?
    a. If so, please do explain

Regarding "Flow" that I mentioned earlier, Drew Brown and I often talk about it, and psycho-philosophical jargon like self-actualization, which would be the point or moments where the Twirler is just creating new moves and wooing the crowd seemingly effortlessly....organically Twirlin'

There is some debate on what Twirlin' should be classified as, and I'm convinced that there will be different genres of Twirlin' suitable for different times and places....Everything from the Hard core tricksters like D Fin and Drew Brown to the smoothest of the smooth like Paco and Franz Hughes, and on to the Speedsters like Zorro and Mike. I've always tried to incorporate transition moves that flow together and a few tricks to cap off a flow, while keeping the speed way up. If I can't do all three of those, I usually avoid adding new moves.

Regarding the cane itself, I like a wooden cane the same length as my right arm. I always remove the stopper. I always add tissue to the tip of the cane and wrap it was electrical tape, so that I can feel the end of cane without thinking about it or adding extra weight. I like the hook to be at least as wide as my closed fist. I never wrap the cane a dark color, always white, so that it can be seen near my dark cloths. Finally, I usually add one strip of tape to the center of gravity on the cane so that I know where to get quick control of it, in a potentially out-of-control situation.

8. Where do you see the skill set in the near and far future? (Please be honest)?

I hope that people keep traveling and trading ideas and using the YouTube videos to push the envelope and eventually make everything that I did look ancient. As I travel I meet lots of younger brothers and women that are discouraged by the YouTube video posters, and they just give up. I hope that I am meeting the exception and that fear isn't the culture of the up and coming cane Twirlers. I'm a realist and reality says that Twirlin' is a dying art form/skill set or whatever we'll call it, and hopefully these interviews and the continued publication of videos and other media will provoke some Twirlin'

9. We'd love to read any other details about your experience that you feel are misunderstood or require greater clarification.

> I'm not sure that I have anything else to add. I would like to say that in my experience, practice makes perfect. When newer Twirlers ask me about how to get "good", I tell them to practice, then I'll see them try and record moves that they've barely got mastered. Any move that is done outside of practice should be executable eight out of ten times, at least.
>
> The best advice I can give to someone just starting, and it may read a bit cliché, is to stop trying to immolate what everyone else if doing, and just be the best at the moves that you'd like to execute. Kanemastery is an exponential set of step-by-step growth every step is important and the growth is noticeably larger than the last.

About the Author

Kwesi is a devoted husband to his wife, Aneesha and a loving father to his two children, Adia Ma'at and Indigo Maasai. He has been a member of Kappa Alpha Psi fraternity Inc. since 2002. In true Kappa fashion, he has pursued high levels of achievement through education, earning a Bachelor of Architecture from Tuskegee University in 2002 and a Master of Architecture from the University of Illinois at Chicago in 2003. He is currently pursuing a Master of Science in Sustainability Management at Columbia University. In addition to being an avid twirler, Kwesi has committed his life to teaching about creating sustainable environments and building sustainable communities. Although he began Twirlin' during his undergraduate years at Tuskegee University, he continues to twirl in order to share the secrets of the art with the next generation and to hone his skills. As he says "There are a lot of secrets waiting to be revealed to any brother willing to *pay the cane*". His passion for sharing the art and history of Twirlin' encouraged this book and it is his hope that others will be inspired to pick up the cane and build upon the stories contained within these pages. Twirlin' is more than an undergraduate experience; it is a bond that endures.

Reference Notes

We are building something new here. There are a few sources to further discover history of Twirlin'. Aside from this physical text, we will be keeping a live archive of Twirlin' history and links at Twirlin Dot Info

>http://twirlin.info
>@TwirlinDotInfo

www.ingramcontent.com/pod-product-compliance
Lightning Source LLC
Chambersburg PA
CBHW062004180426
43198CB00036B/2327